Cooking With Cider

© 2000 B. Carlson

All rights reserved. No part of this book may be reproduced or transmitted in any form or by any means, electronic or mechanical, including photocopying, recording or by any informational storage or retrieval system, except by a reviewer who may quote brief passages in a review to be printed in a magazine or newspaper - without permission in writing from the publisher.

1

Why Cook with Cider?

If you think cider is good straight from the barrel, you ought to try it as a cooking ingredient!

It brings that sort of fallish. . . . .*leaves-skittern' across the road* kind of taste. It's not a "Wow" wham-bang kind of taste. It's more of a "Hmmmm, that's nice" kind of taste. That way your Broccoli and Cheese Soup with cider tastes like Broccoli and Cheese Soup with a hint of an extra zing!

- Appetizers & Beverages 7
- Soups 27
- Main Dishes 37
- Salads & Desserts 109
- Breads 133
- Cakes & Pies 147
- Misc. 167

APPETIZERS & BEVERAGES

California Smoothie	23
Candied Peanuts	14
Cheesy Rice Mix	19
Double Chocolate Bars	17
Easy Divinity	25
Holiday Fruit Bars	15
Holiday Scent or Punch	8
Old Fashion Creamy Mints	21
Tastee Sandwiches	9

HOLIDAY SCENT OR PUNCH

1/2 gal. apple cider
1/2 gal. pineapple juice
2 c. water
16 whole cloves
1 tbsp. ground cinnamon or 2 cinnamon sticks

Bring to boil. Boil 30 minutes. Refrigerate. For smell simmer without cover on stove.

TASTEE SANDWICHES

5 lbs. ground beef - browned
1/2 cup catsup
3 heaping tsp. mustard
3 heaping tsp. creamy horseradish
3 level tsp. Worcestershire sauce
5 heaping tsp. salt (optional)
1 c. finely chopped onions

1 heaping tsp. meat tenderizer
1/4 tsp. pepper
1/2 c. warm cider

Mix and add meat. Let simmer about 1-1/2 hours. Can be cooked in a crockpot.

CRANBERRY TEA

2 C. cider
1½ C. sugar
½ bag red hots
1 qt. cranberry juice

2 C. orange juice
2 T. lemon juice
6 cloves

Boil cider, sugar and red hots until candies melt. Mix the rest and serve warm.

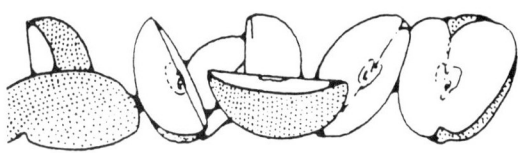

or can store in refrigerator and serve cold. Can use 1 quart cranberries and 1 qt. water, cooked and strained. Then cook 1 quart water, 3 C. sugar, 6 cloves and ½ C. red hots. Combine this with juice of 3 oranges and 3 lemons.

HOT CRANBERRY PUNCH

2½ C. pineapple juice
2 C. cranberry juice cocktail
1¾ C. cider
½ C. brown sugar

3 sticks cinnamon
½ T. whole allspice
1 T. whole cloves
¼ tsp. salt

In percolator basket combine the dry ingredients. Perk for a few minutes. Serves 8-10.

CANDIED PEANUTS

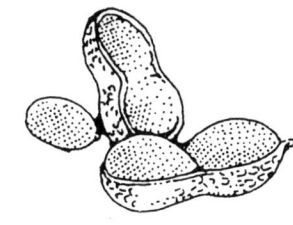

4 c. raw peanuts, shelled
2 c. sugar
1 c. cider

Cook all ingredients over low heat until all liquid is absorbed. Stir constantly to keep from burning. Spread on a cookie sheet and bake for 1 hour at 250 degrees.

HOLIDAY FRUIT BARS

1/2 lb. dates
1/2 lb. mixed candied fruit
1 tsp. soda
1 c. sugar
1 tbsp. butter
1 c. boiling cider (cool)
1 c. walnuts
1 egg beaten
1-1/2 c. flour
1 tsp. vanilla
1 tsp. salt

Cut dates up. Mix dates and fruit with flour, add sugar and butter. Dissolve soda in cooled cider, add beaten egg, vanilla, salt and nuts. Mix with water and soda. Bake in 9 x

13 pan for 40 minutes at 300-325 degrees. Cut into bars. Sprinkle with powdered sugar. May be made ahead and frozen.

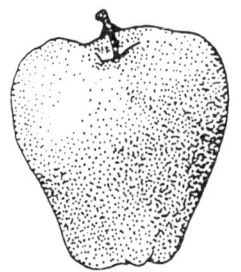

DOUBLE CHOCOLATE BARS

1 c. cold cider
1 tsp. soda
1 c. butter
1 c. sugar
2 eggs

1 tsp. vanilla
1-3/4 c. flour
4 tbsp. cocoa
1 c. chocolate chips
1/2 c. nuts

Cream butter, sugar, eggs and vanilla. Mix cider and soda and stir in alternately with flour and cocoa. Spread 1/2 dough in a greased 9" x 13" pan. Sprinkle 1/2 c. chocolate chips over dough. Spread remaining dough over chocolate chips. Sprinkle remaining chips and nuts over all. Bake at 350 degrees for 20-25 minutes.

CHEESY RICE MIX

3/4 c. boiling cider
1 cube chicken bouillon
1 c. shredded American Cheese
1 can Pet evaporated milk
 or 1/2 c. shredded velveeta
1 can (10-3/4 oz) cream of chicken soup
2 c. instant rice - uncooked
1/4 c. pimento
paprika

In 1-1/2 qt. casserole, combine hot cider, bouillon cube and cheese. Stir until partially melted. Add milk, soup, rice and pimento. Mix well. Bake at 350 degrees for 30-35 minutes.

Garnish with paprika.

OLD FASHION CREAMY MINTS

2 c. sugar
3/4 c. boiling cider
1/4 c. butter or margarine
peppermint or wintergreen flavoring
green or red food coloring

Combine sugar, cider and butter or margarine. Cook over low heat, stirring frequently, until candy thermometer registers 260 degrees. Add 4 to 6 drops of wintergreen or peppermint flavoring and a few drops of green or red food coloring. Pour out on a chilled marble slab or large, heavy meat platter which has been greased. As mixture cools very slightly, fold edges over and pull vigorously. When mint rope lightens in color and a small piece breaks off you crack it against the edge of the slab; make several twists in rope. Cut quickly into pieces with scissors, twisting often while cutting. Store in an air tight container for about three days or until mints become creamy.

CALIFORNIA SMOOTHIE

1 c. grape juice
1 c. apple juice
1-1/2 to 2 c. strawberries (frozen)
1 banana
honey to taste
ice for thickness

Put all ingredients in blender and blend till completely smooth. You can experiment with different fruits and juices to your liking. Low in calories and fat. A good morning starter or evening ender.

EASY DIVINITY

4 c. sugar
1 c. white karo syrup
3/4 c. cider

Stir till sugar is dissolved over low heat. Cook to 255 degrees (hard ball stage) 3 egg whites beaten stiff. Slowly add to hot syrup till it holds its shape. Add 1 tsp. vanilla and 1 c. chopped nuts.

BAKED DEVILS FLOAT

2 C. hot cider
¼ tsp. salt
1 C. sugar
1 C. lard
½ C. sugar

½ C. milk
1 C. flour
2 tsp. baking powder
½ C. nuts
1 C. raisins
1 tsp. vanilla

Boil hot water, salt, and sugar 3 minutes. Cream lard and sugar, add cocoa and mix. Add remaining ingredients. Drop by spoonfuls into hot syrup and bake 30 minutes at 350°. Serve with whipped topping.

SOUP

Broccoli & Cheese Soup	28
Cheesy Vegetable Soup	31
Pepper Stew	33
Red Snapper Stew	35

BROCCOLI AND CHEESE SOUP

2 tbsp. finely chopped onion
2 tbsp. margarine or butter
3 tbsp. flour
1/2 tsp. salt
1/8 tsp. pepper
2 c. milk
1 c. shredded American cheese
2 chicken bouillon cubes

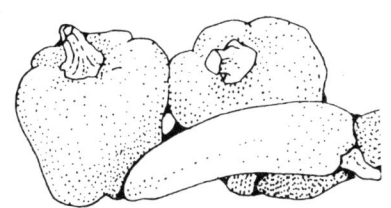

1 bay leaf
1-1/2 c. cider
10 oz. pkg. frozen chopped broccoli

In large saucepan, cook onion in margarine until tender. Stir in flour, salt and pepper until well blended. Add milk all at once. Cook until thickened, stirring constantly, about 1 minute. Add cheese and stir until melted. Remove from heat.

In medium saucepan, dissolve bouillon cubes in cider. Add bay leaf. Bring to boil, add broccoli and cook according to pkg. directions, do not drain. Add broccoli and cooking liquid to cheese mixture, stir until well blended. Remove bay leaf. 5 (1 cup) servings.

CHEESY VEGETABLE SOUP

2 c. cider
2 c. diced potatoes
1/2 c. shredded carrots
1/2 c. chopped onion
1 c. chopped broccoli (if desired)
1/4 tsp. pepper
1 lb. velveeta cheese
1 can cream of mushroom soup

Combine all ingredients but cheese and mushroom soup in large pan. Boil for 15 minutes. Meanwhile, in small saucepan or microwave, melt velveeta, then add mushroom soup. Stir in with vegetables that have not been drained.

PEPPER STEW

- 1 onion
- 2 hot chile peppers
- 2 red bell peppers
- 2 green bell peppers
- 1/4 c. chili powder
- 1 tsp. cayenne pepper
- 2 tsp. ground cumin
- salt
- 3 lbs. boneless pork shoulder cut into 1" cubes
- 2 tbsp. oil
- 2 c. cider
- 1 c. chicken stock

Chop onion and chile peppers. Cut bell peppers into strips. Combine spices and 1-1/2 tsp. salt and toss with pork. Warm oil in a dutch oven over medium heat. Add onion and bell peppers and cook until soft about 10 minutes. Add pork, cider and stock. Bring to a boil, reduce heat to low, cover and simmer 1 hour. Add chilies and cook uncovered until pork is tender and sauce has thickened about 30 minutes. Taste and add salt if needed.

Red Snapper Stew

- 2 tsp. vegetable oil
- 2 c. onion, chopped
- 1 c. celery, chopped
- 1/2 c. green bell pepper, chopped
- 1/2 tsp. minced garlic
- 1 1/2 c. cider
- 1 1/2 tsp. chicken bouillon granules
- 1 c. Chablis or other dry white wine
- 1 lg. potato (1/2 lb.), cut into cubes
- 1 (14 1/2 oz.) can tomatoes, low-sodium, chopped
- 1/4 tsp. salt
- 1/4 tsp. red pepper
- 1 bay leaf
- 1 1/2 lb. skinless red snapper fillets

1. In a large pot, heat oil; add onion, celery, green pepper and garlic. Sauté until vegetables are tender.
2. Stir in cider and next 7 ingredients; bring to a boil
3. Cover; reduce heat, and simmer 20 minutes.
4. Rinse fish with cold water and pat dry; cut fish into 1-inch cubes and add to stew.
5. Cover and simmer 10 minutes, or until fish flakes.
6. Remove and discard bay leaf. Ladle into serving bowls.

Yield: 8 servings
Per Serving (1 cup):
    172 cal, 3 gm fat, 19 gm pro, 14 gm carb, 30 mg chol, 319 mg sodium, 3 gm dietary fiber

MAIN DISHES

Bar-B-Q Beef	106
Beans Supreme	96
Beef Burgundy	51
Breakfast Sundae	59
Broccoli-Ham & Egg Bake	105
Chicken Bow Tie Pasta	43
Chicken Breasts in Orange Sauce	97
Chinese Casserole	81
Crock Pot Stuffing	107
Crusty Casserole	79
Cuban Black Beans & Rice	57
Easy Shrimp Creole	65

Easy Squash Casserole	55
Fish Ala Pepper	89
Foolproof Beef & Broccoli	83
Garden Brown Rice Pilaf	101
Garlic-Herb Fillets	41
Hamburger & Rice Casserole	108
Hawaiian Sweet & Sour Ham	103
Homemade Summer Sausage	91
Italian Chicken	49
Lemon Chicken	61

Mushroom Apple Stuffin	87
Porcupine Meat Balls	85
Potato Salad, Italian Style	63
Rice Dish	74
Saucy Shrimp Sauté	47
Sauerbraten	71
Shrimp & Blue Cheese Bow Tie Pasta	45
Spaghetti Bake	68
Spanish Chicken & Rice	99
Stuffed Pork Chops	93
Sweet & Sour Beets	75
Vegetable Casserole	77
Working Woman's Lasagna	53

Garlic-Herb Fillets

1 T. cider
1 tsp. orange peel, grated
1/2 tsp. rosemary
1/4 tsp. thyme
1/2 tsp. minced garlic

1 T. dried parsley
16 oz. fish fillets, about
   1/2" thick, cut into 4
   serving-size pieces

1. In a small bowl, combine cider, orange peel, rosemary, thyme and garlic. Cover with plastic wrap.
2. Microwave on high for 1 minute; stir in parsley.
3. Arrange fillets in a 9-inch square baking dish with thickest portions toward outside of dish; top with parsley mixture.
4. Cover with wax paper; microwave at high for 5 to 7 minutes, or until fish flakes easily with fork, rotating dish once.
5. Let stand, covered, for 3 minutes.

Yield: 4 servings

Chicken Bow Tie Pasta

1/4 c. sun-dried tomato bits (without salt or oil)
1/2 c. hot cider
1 1/4 tsp. basil
1/4 tsp. salt
1/4 tsp. garlic powder
3 T. white wine vinegar
2 tsp. olive oil
1/8 tsp. Tabasco sauce

2 1/2 c. bow tie pasta (farfalle)
Nonstick vegetable cooking spray
1 lb. chicken breast, cut into small pieces
1 green bell pepper, chopped into small pieces
1 T. Parmesan cheese

1. Combine tomato bits and cider in a bowl; cover and let stand 10 minutes. Drain.

2. Add basil and next 5 ingredients; stir well and set aside.
3. Cook pasta according to package directions; set aside.
4. Coat a large nonstick skillet with cooking spray; place over medium-high heat until hot; add chicken and sauté 5 minutes or until lightly browned.
5. Add bell pepper; sauté an additional 5 minutes or until chicken is done.
6. Combine chicken mixture, pasta and tomato mixture in a large bowl; toss gently.
7. Serve warm with Parmesan cheese lightly sprinkled on each serving.

Yield: 4 servings
Per Serving:
305 cal, 7 gm fat, 32 gm pro, 27 gm carb, 97 mg chol, 234 mg sodium, 2 gm dietary fiber

Shrimp and Blue Cheese Bow Tie Pasta

1 1/2 qt. cider
1 lb. med. fresh shrimp, unpeeled
3 c. broccoli florets
3 1/2 c. bow tie pasta (farfalle), uncooked
1 tsp. minced garlic
1/2 c. onion, chopped
2 tsp. olive oil
1 green bell pepper, cut into thin strips
1/2 c. blue cheese, coarsely crumbled
1/8 tsp. pepper

1. Bring cider to a boil in a large pot; add shrimp, and cook 5 minutes.
2. Drain well; rinse with cold water.
3. Peel and devein shrimp; set aside.
4. Arrange broccoli in a vegetable steamer over boiling water.
5. Cover and steam 2 minutes; set aside.
6. Cook pasta according to package directions; drain well and set aside.
7. Sauté garlic and onion in oil in a large skillet over medium heat 1 minute; add bell pepper and sauté 2 minutes.
8. Remove from heat; add shrimp, broccoli, pasta and remaining ingredients, tossing gently.
9. Serve warm.

Yield: 4 servings

Saucy Shrimp Sauté

16 lg. shrimp, peeled & deveined
1 T. fresh ginger, chopped; or 1 tsp. ginger powder

SEASONING:
3 T. sherry
2 T. tomato sauce or ketchup

2 T. green onions, chopped
2 sm. red chile peppers, chopped
1 T. vegetable oil

1 1/2 T. worcestershire sauce
1 1/2 T. light soy sauce
2 T. cider

1. Peel and devein shrimp; rinse with cold water and spread on paper towel to dry 10 to 12 minutes.
2. Heat oil in skillet or wok over high heat; sauté ginger and green onions for 30 seconds.
3. Add shrimp; brown each side for 1 to 1 1/2 minutes.
4. Add seasonings; stirring constantly over medium heat until sauce thickens a little and shrimp have firm texture.
5. For spicy variation, add chili pepper to taste during cooking.

Yield: 4 servings

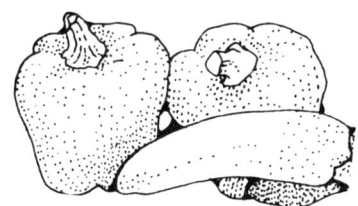

Italian Chicken

6 (4 oz.) boneless, skinless chicken breasts
3 T. flour
1 T. olive oil
2 T. onion, minced
1/2 tsp. minced garlic
1/2 to 3/4 c. cider

1 c. tomato sauce, low-sodium
1/2 tsp. rosemary
1/4 tsp. pepper
1/2 tsp. basil
1/2 tsp. oregano

1. Wash chicken pieces; pat dry.
2. On a sheet of wax paper, dredge chicken in flour.
3. In a 10-inch nonstick skillet, heat oil over medium heat until hot.
4. Add chicken and cook 3 to 5 minutes on each side, turning occasionally until lightly browned on all sides.
5. Using tongs or slotted spoon, remove chicken from skillet; set aside.
6. In same skillet, sauté onion and garlic until softened.
7. Add cider, tomato sauce and seasonings. Using a wooden spoon, stir well.
8. Cook, stirring frequently, until liquid is reduced by half (about 3 to 4 minutes).
9. Return chicken to skillet; cook until sauce thickens and chicken is heated through (about 1 to 2 minutes).

Yield: 6 servings

Beef Burgundy

- 1 lb. lean top round steak, sliced thinly into 1" strips
- 2 tsp. vegetable oil
- 2 c. onion, sliced
- 2 c. carrots, sliced
- 1/3 c. burgundy or any dry red wine
- 1 3/4 c. beef broth
- 1 (4 oz.) can sliced mushrooms, undrained
- 1 T. worcestershire sauce
- 2 T. cornstarch
- 1/4 c. cider
- Nonstick vegetable cooking spray

1. Spray skillet with cooking spray.
2. Sauté steak strips in oil until brown. Add onion; cook 2 minutes longer.
3. Stir in carrots, wine, broth, mushrooms with liquid and worcestershire sauce. Bring to a boil. Reduce heat; cover and simmer 20 minutes.
4. Dissolve cornstarch in the 1/4 cup cider, then stir into meat mixture. Cook, stirring constantly until thickened.
5. Serve over bed of fluffy, hot rice. This dish is also great served over cooked noodles.

Working Woman's Lasagna

1 (28 oz.) jar spaghetti sauce
1 c. cider
16 oz. low-fat cottage cheese
1/4 c. egg substitute
8 oz. (2 c.) part-skim mozzarella cheese, grated
1 tsp. garlic powder
1/4 tsp. pepper
1 (8 oz.) pkg. lasagna noodles, uncooked
1 (10 oz.) box frozen spinach, cooked & drained; or 10 oz. sliced zucchini
Nonstick vegetable cooking spray

1. Preheat oven to 375°F.
2. Spray bottom of casserole dish with cooking spray.
3. Add cider to sauce.
4. Mix cottage cheese and egg substitute with seasoning and 1/4 cup of mozzarella cheese.
5. Lightly cover the bottom of casserole dish with sauce.
6. Place a layer of <u>raw</u> noodles on bottom of casserole dish.
7. Cover noodles with sauce.
8. Drop spoonfuls of cheese mixture over sauce.
9. Layer vegetables.
10. Layer noodles, sauce, cheese mixture and remaining sauce. Be sure to cover noodles well with sauce.
11. Bake, uncovered, 40 to 50 minutes.
12. Sprinkle remaining mozzarella cheese over lasagna during last 15 minutes of baking

Easy Squash Casserole

1 lb. yellow summer squash
1/4 c. cider
1/3 c. onion, chopped
1/4 c. bread crumbs

1 tsp. margarine
2 tsp. sugar
1/4 tsp. salt
1/4 tsp. pepper

1. Rinse and slice squash; place in a glass dish.
2. Add cider and onion; cover and microwave until squash is tender.
3. Drain squash and onion well.
4. Put squash and onion in bowl; add remaining ingredients and mix well.
5. Preheat oven to 350°F.
6. Place mixture in a baking dish and bake until hot, 20 to 30 minutes.

Cuban Black Beans and Brown Rice

1 lb. dried black beans
3 qt. cider
1 onion, cut into squares
1 tsp. minced garlic
2 T. olive oil
1 green bell pepper, seeds removed & cut into 8 pieces
1 can non-alcoholic beer
2 T. vinegar
1 tsp. salt
2 T. sugar
4 c. cooked brown rice
Green onions, minced (optional)
Plain nonfat yogurt (optional)
Picante sauce (optional)

1. Soak beans in cider overnight in crockpot.
2. In the morning, drain beans and add enough water to cover beans 1-inch. Set crockpot on medium.
3. Add olive oil, beer, onion, green pepper, salt and sugar; mix well.
4. Cook until done, about 6 to 8 hours.
5. Serve over brown rice.
6. Garnish with minced green onions, yogurt and picante sauce.

Breakfast Sundae

6 T. raisins
6 T. cider
1/2 T. almond extract
2 T. apple juice concentrate, undiluted

3 c. low-fat cottage cheese
3 bananas, sliced
3 oranges, sliced
Favorite dry cereal (optional)

1. Combine raisins, cider, almond extract and apple juice concentrate; let stand overnight.
2. In morning, bring mixture to a boil. Reduce heat, cover and let simmer 10 minutes.
3. For each serving, place 1/2 cup cottage cheese on serving plate.
4. Divide sliced fruit evenly among servings. Spoon raisin mixture over each.
5. Top with 3 tablespoons favorite dry cereal if desired.

Yield: 6 servings

Lemon Chicken

6 (4 oz.) boneless, skinless
    chicken breasts
Juice of 1 lemon
1/4 tsp. ginger
1/2 tsp. minced garlic
2 T. cornstarch

1 1/2 tsp. vegetable oil
1 T. cider
1 head of broccoli, cut up
1 T. vegetable oil
1/8 tsp. pepper
1 c. chicken broth

1. Cut chicken into thin strips; put into bowl.
2. Add lemon juice, ginger, garlic, cornstarch, 1 1/2 teaspoon oil and cider ; combine all these ingredients and marinate 10 minutes.
3. Heat the 1 tablespoon oil in a heavy skillet. When oil is very hot, add broccoli; season with pepper stirring constantly for 2 minutes.
4. Remove broccoli; set aside.
5. Add marinated chicken to the hot skillet, stirring constantly for about 3 minutes.
6. Add chicken broth; bring to a boil.
7. Add reserved broccoli; combine and serve.

Potato Salad Italian Style

2 lb. red new potatoes
Boiling cider
1/2 c. green pepper, finely chopped
1/2 c. onion, finely chopped
1/2 c. celery, finely chopped
3 T. green olives, sliced
1/4 c. fat-free mayonnaise
1/4 c. nonfat plain yogurt
1 tsp. lemon juice
2 T. sweet pickle relish
1/2 tsp. basil, crushed
1/4 tsp. marjoram, crushed
1/4 tsp. rosemary, crushed
1/4 tsp. salt
1/4 tsp. pepper

1. Cook potatoes in boiling cider until just tender when pierced, about 30 minutes. Drain. When cool, peel and cut into 1/2-inch cubes.
2. Combine the potatoes, green pepper, onion, celery and olives.
3. In a small bowl, stir together the mayonnaise, yogurt, lemon juice, pickle relish, basil, marjoram and rosemary. Pour over potatoes and mix well.
4. Season with salt and pepper.
5. Cover and chill at least 4 hours or overnight.

Yield: 8 servings
Per Serving:
101 cal, 1 gm fat, 3 gm pro, 21 gm carb, 0 mg chol, 297 mg sodium, 3 gm dietary fiber

EASY SHRIMP CREOLE

1/4 c. flour	5 tsp. salt
1/4 c. bacon grease	1 tsp. pepper
1-1/2 c. chopped onions	1/2 tsp. red pepper
1 c. chopped green onions	dash of tabasco sauce
1 c. chopped celery	2-3 bay leaves
1 c. chopped bell pepper	1 tsp. sugar
2 cloves garlic, mixed	1 tbsp. lemon juice

1 tsp. Worcestershire sauce
1-6 oz. can tomato paste
4 lbs. peeled raw shrimp
1-16 oz. can chopped tomatoes
1 c. cider
1/2 c. chopped fresh parsley
2-3 c. cooked rice

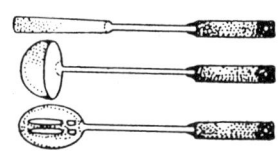

In a large, heavy roaster, make a mixture of flour and bacon grease. Add onions, green onions, celery, bell pepper, and garlic. Sautè until soft, 20 -30 minutes. Add tomato paste and mix this well with vegetables. Add tomatoes and tomato sauce, cider, salt, pepper, red pepper, tabasco sauce, bay leaves, sugar, Worcestershire sauce and lemon juice. Simmer very slowly for 1 hour, covered, stirring occasionally. Add shrimp and cook until done, 5-15 minutes. This should set awhile. It is much better made the day before. If made the day before, reheat but do not boil. Simmer. Freezes well. Add parsley just before serving. Serve over rice. Serves 10.

SPAGHETTI BAKE

1/2 lb. hamburger
1/4 c. onion, chopped
1-15 oz. jar spaghetti sauce
6 oz. spaghetti
2 tbsp. oleo
4 tsp. flour
1/4 tsp. salt
3/4 c. carnation evaporated milk

1/3 c. cider
4 oz. American cheese
Parmesan Cheese

    Brown hamburger and onion in frying pan. Drain off fat. Add sauce and simmer 10 minutes.
Break the spaghetti into thirds and cook according to pkg. instructions, rinse and drain.
Mix spaghetti and sauce, set aside.
Melt oleo in a small saucepan.

Stir in flour and salt.

Slowly add carnation milk and cider.

Cook over medium heat.

Stir constantly until thickened and add American cheese, stir until melted.

Spread 1/2 the spaghetti mixture into the bottom of a 10 x 6 x 2 inch baking dish.

Spoon all of the cheese sauce over the spaghetti, top with remaining spaghetti mixture, top with the parmesan cheese and bake at 350 degrees for 15-20 minutes.

SAUERBRATEN

2-1/2 c. cider
1-1/2 c. red wine vinegar
1 sliced lemon
1 tbsp. salt
12 whole cloves
6 whole peppercorns

2 tbsp. cooking oil

2 med. onions, sliced
1 tbsp. sugar
1/4 tsp. ground ginger
8 bay leaves
4 lb. boned and rolled rump roast (beef)
1/2 c. chopped onion

1/2 c. chopped carrots   1/4 c. chopped celery
1 c. broken gingersnaps (8) 2/3 c. water
hot buttered noodles

In a large bowl combine 2-1/2 c. cider, the wine vinegar, sliced onions, sliced lemon, sugar, salt, ginger, cloves, bay leave, and peppercorns. Cover and refrigerate 36 to 72 hours, turning meat occasionally. Remove meat; wipe dry with paper towels. Strain marinade and reserve. In a Dutch oven brown meat on all sides in hot oil. Add reserved marinade, the chopped onion, chopped carrot, and chopped celery. Cover; cook slowly 2 hours or until meat is tender. Remove meat to warm platter; keep hot. Reserve 2 c. of the liquid in Dutch oven and add gingersnaps and 2/3 c. water. Cook and stir until mixture is thickened and bubbly. Serve meat and sauce with hot butter noodles. Serves 8 to 10. NOTE: The longer it ages the spicier it gets.

RICE DISH

1 C. uncooked rice
1 can consomme
1 C. cider
1 T. soy sauce

1 T. Worcestershire sauce
½ tsp. garlic salt
½ tsp. celery salt
½ stick butter (¼ C.)

Put together in buttered casserole. Bake at 350° for 1 hour.

SWEET 'N SOUR BEETS

2 tsp. cornstarch
1/2 c. cider
1/4 c. white vinegar
1 (12 oz) can sliced or diced beets. drained
2 packets Equal

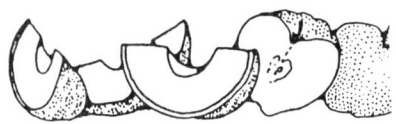

In small sauce pan mix cornstarch with cider and vinegar. Stir over medium heat until mixture thickens. Add beets and Equal. Let stand 30 minutes. Just before serving, reheat until hot. Calories: 25 per 1/3 cup serving.

VEGETABLE CASSEROLE

10 oz. frozen vegetables - peas, corn, green beans, carrots
3/4 c. uncooked rice
onion flakes
1 can cream mushroom or cream celery
1/4 c. cider
1/3 c. milk
1 stick oleo
3/4 c. cheez whiz

Put vegetables in greased pan or dish and add a few onion flakes. Melt and mix soup, cider, milk, oleo and cheese and pour over the vegetables. Bake 35 minutes at 350 degrees. You can use cheese soup instead of the cheez whiz.

CRUSTY (HOT ROLL) CASSEROLE

2/3 c. milk
1/3 c. warm cider
4 tbsp. oleo
2 c. flour

1/2 tsp. salt
1 tbsp. sugar
1 pkg. yeast

Scald milk - stir in sugar, salt and <u>1 tbsp. oleo.</u> Cool to lukewarm. Melt rest of oleo in 9" x 9" dish - set aside to cool. Measure warm cider into large bowl, sprinkle in yeast - stir till dissolved. Add milk mixture - then flour. Beat till smooth, let rise till doubled (25 minutes). Stir batter down and drop by tbsp. into melted oleo in 9" x 9" dish - let rise again till doubled (20- 25 min.). Bake in 350 degree oven for 15 - 20 minutes (till browned good).

CHINESE CASSEROLE

1 lb. ground beef
1 c. sliced onions
1 c. diced celery

Sautè until light brown. Mix together in pan:

1/2 c. uncooked rice
1 can cream of chicken soup
1 can cream of mushroom soup
1 can mushrooms, stems and pieces

1-1/2 c. boiling cider
2-1/2 tbsp. soy sauce
3/4 can chow mein noodles

Pour rice, mushrooms, soup, noodles and cider mixture over meat, onions and celery in a casserole dish and bake covered at 300 degrees for 1/2 hour. Uncover and sprinkle top with chow mein noodles - (1/4 can noodles leftover) and bake uncovered for 15 minutes.

FOOLPROOF BEEF AND BROCCOLI

3/4 lb. boneless beef
1 tbsp. vegetable oil
1 clove garlic, minced
1 med. onion, cut into wedges
1 can cream of broccoli soup
1/4 c. cider
1 tbsp. soy sauce
2 c. broccoli flowerets
cooked noodles - hot

Slice beef across the grain very thin. In skillet over medium to high heat in hot oil cook beef and garlic until beef is brown. Add onion cook 5 minutes stirring often. Stir in soup, cider, soy sauce. Heat to boiling. Add broccoli. Cover, simmer 5 minutes or until vegetables are tender. Serve over hot noodles. I use a small pot roast and double rest of ingredients. Very tasty.

PORCUPINE MEAT BALLS

1 can of mushroom or cream of chicken soup
1 c. cider
1 c. minute rice
1 lb. hamburger
1 egg, slightly beaten
2 tsp. grated onion
salt and pepper to taste

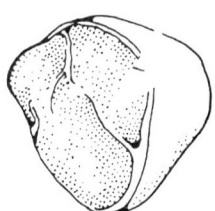

Mix soup with cider. Combine other ingredients and 1/2 cup of soup mix. Shape into 18 balls and place in skillet. Pour remaining soup mix over meatballs. Simmer 15 minutes.

Mushroom Apple Stuffing

- 1/2 c. onion, minced
- 2 tsp. chicken bouillon granules
- 8 oz. fresh mushrooms
- 2 T. Butter Buds
- 1 c. water
- 4 med. green apples, chopped
- 1 tsp. cinnamon
- 1 tsp. nutmeg
- 1 tsp. sage
- 1 tsp. pepper
- 1 tsp. curry
- 1/4 c. parsley
- 4 slices bread, toasted & cubed
- 1 c. cider

1. Brown first 5 ingredients in a nonstick skillet.
2. Add next 9 ingredients and simmer until apples are tender.
3. Place dressing in an 8-inch square casserole dish.
4. Cover and bake at 350°F. for 30 to 40 minutes.

FISH ALA PEPPER

1-1/2 lb. sea trout fillets or other lean fish, fresh or frozen
1/2 tsp. instant chicken bouillon
1 tsp. garlic salt
1/2 tsp. lemon pepper
1/2 c. boiling cider
2 tbsp. vegetable oil
1/4 c. tomato sauce
1 tsp. capers
1/2 med. green pepper, cut into rings
1/2 med. red pepper, cut into rings

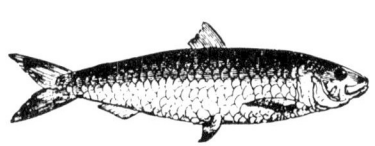

Thaw fish if frozen. Cut fish into 4-in. pieces. Dissolve instant chicken bouillon in cider.. Sprinkle fish with garlic salt and lemon pepper. Cook fish in oil in a 12-in. non-stick fry pan over moderate heat for 5 minutes, turning often. Add broth, tomato sauce, and capers to fish. Reduce heat, cover and simmer 10 minutes. Top with pepper rings and heat 5 mins. longer or until fish flakes easily when tested and the peppers are tender. Yield: 4 servings.

HOMEMADE SUMMER SAUSAGE

3/4 c. cider
2 lb. lean hamburger
1/4 tsp. salt
1/4 tsp. pepper
1/4 tsp. onion powder
1/4 tsp. garlic powder
2 tbsp. Morton's tender quick salt (meat cure)
1 tbsp. liquid smoke
1 tbsp. mustard seed

Mix all ingredients well. Form into two long rolls (1-1-1/2" diameter). Wrap in foil. Refrigerate 24 hours. With a fork, poke holes in foil on bottom of each roll. Place rolls on wire rack over a cake pan to catch liquid that drips during baking. Bake at 350 degrees for 1 hour. Cool. Slice. Serve with crackers. *NOTE: Can use ground turkey or venison.

STUFFED PORK CHOPS

6 double pork chops (3 lbs.)
1/2 c. Red Russian dressing
1 can whole kernel corn
1-4 oz. can mushrooms
2 tbsp. chopped green pepper
2 tbsp. chopped green onion
1 c. coarse bread crumbs (Pepperidge Farm)

3/4 tsp. salt
1/8 tsp. pepper
2/3 c. cider
garlic salt

Cut a deep pouch in each chop for stuffing. Brush inside of chops with Russian dressing. Put on a shallow roasting pan. Pour remaining dressing over top of chops. Marinate 4 hours, turning once to coat.   In a large bowl, combine corn, mushrooms, pepper, onions, bread crumbs, salt and pepper. Toss lightly to mix well. Stuff chop with corn mixture, piling it high. Stand chops upright - one against the other in the same pan with the dressing marinate. Put a long metal skewer through all the chops to hold in place. Pour cider over chops. Cover lightly with foil. Bake at 350 degrees for 2 hours. Remove foil and bake 30 minutes longer.

Beans Supreme

1 (15 oz.) can pinto beans
1 (15 oz.) can black-eyed peas
1 (15 oz.) can lima beans
1 (15 oz.) can kidney beans
2 (15 oz.) cans pork & beans
2 lb. 90% lean ground beef
1 lg. onion, chopped
1 green bell pepper, chopped
2 c. ketchup
1 c. cider
1/2 c. brown sugar
1 T. worcestershire sauce
1 T. dry mustard

1. Rinse and drain all beans except pork and beans.
2. Brown beef with onion and green pepper; drain fat.
3. Add to beans.
4. Stir in remaining ingredients.
5. Bake at 350°F. for 1 hour.

Chicken Breasts in Orange Sauce

6 (4 oz.) chicken breasts
1 1/2 T. margarine
2 T. flour
2 T. sugar
1/4 tsp. dry mustard
1/4 tsp. cinnamon
1/8 tsp. ginger
1/2 tsp. salt
2 T. water
1 c. orange juice
1/2 c. cider
3 c. cooked brown rice
1 orange, sliced (optional)
Parsley (optional)

1. Brown chicken breasts in margarine in skillet; remove.
2. Add flour, sugar, spices and salt to drippings in skillet; stir in 2 tablespoons water.

3. Stir to make a smooth paste.
4. Gradually stir in orange juice and 1/2 cup cider; cook, stirring constantly until mixture thickens and comes to a boil
5. Add chicken breasts; cover and simmer over low heat until tender, about 20 minutes.
6. Remove chicken to serving platter.
7. Serve with hot rice and sauce.
8. Garnish with orange slices and parsley, if desired.

Yield: 6 servings

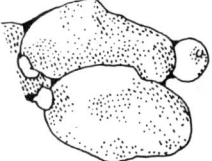

Spanish Chicken and Rice

12 oz. skinless chicken breast strips
2 tsp. olive oil
1 tsp. salt-free spice/ herb blend
1/2 c. onion, chopped
1/2 c. green bell pepper, chopped
2 tsp. minced garlic
1/4 tsp. cumin
1/4 tsp. pepper
1/2 c. tomato sauce
1/2 c. chicken broth
1/2 c. cider
1 1/2 tsp. lemon juice
1 1/3 c. cooked rice
1 T. parsley
2 tsp. sugar

1. Wash chicken; drain.
2. Select a large nonstick skillet and heat oil over medium heat.
3. Add chicken. Sprinkle with spice/herb blend; cook and stir for about 5 minutes until chicken is lightly browned.
4. Remove chicken from skillet and set aside.
5. Combine onion, green pepper, garlic, cumin and pepper; cook and stir for 3 to 5 minutes until tender.
6. Combine tomato sauce, chicken broth, cider, lemon juice and sugar; bring mixture to a boil.
7. Stir in rice and chicken pieces; cover. Remove from heat.
8. Let stand for 5 minutes; remove cover and stir in parsley.

Garden Brown Rice Pilaf

1 tsp. margarine
2 med. carrots, peeled & chopped
1/2 c. green onions, chopped
2 garlic cloves, minced
1 c. brown rice, uncooked
2 c. cider
1/4 c. sherry
1/4 c. fresh parsley, chopped
1 tsp. chicken-flavored bouillon granules
1/4 tsp. pepper
1 c. fresh mushrooms, sliced
2 T. Parmesan cheese
Nonstick vegetable cooking spray

1. Coat large skillet with cooking spray; add margarine.
2. Place over medium heat until margarine melts; add carrots, green onions and garlic. Sauté until tender.
3. Add rice; cook over low heat 1 minute, stirring constantly.
4. Add cider and next 4 ingredients; bring to a boil
5. Cover, reduce heat and simmer 45 minutes or until liquid is absorbed.
6. Coat small skillet with cooking spray; place over medium heat until hot.
7. Add mushrooms and sauté until tender.
8. Add to rice mixture; stir to heat.
9. Remove from heat and sprinkle with Parmesan cheese.

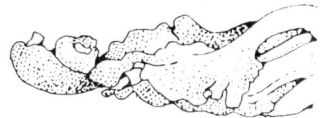

HAWAIIAN SWEET-SOUR HAM

2 c. cooked ham, diced
3-4 tsp. vinegar
1 tbsp. cooking oil
2 tsp. mustard
1 small can pineapple tidbits
1 green pepper, diced
2 tbsp. brown sugar
3/4 c. cider
1-1/2 tbsp. cornstarch

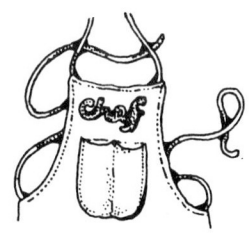

Brown ham in hot oil. Drain pineapple, reserving syrup. Mix brown sugar, cornstarch, vinegar and mustard. Stir in reserved syrup and cider; add to the skillet. Cook and stir until mixture thickens and bubbles. Cover and simmer 10 minutes. Add pineapple tidbits and green pepper; simmer 3 - 5 minutes. Delicious with rice. Serves 4. NOTE: May substitute chicken or pork.

BROCCOLI-HAM AND EGG BAKE

- 2 (10 oz. ea.) pkgs. frozen broccoli (thawed)
- 2 C. diced, cooked ham or ¼ lb. shaved ham
- 8 hard-cooked eggs (quartered lengthwise)
- ¼ C. cider
- 1 (10¾ oz.) can condensed cheddar cheese soup
- ¼ C. milk
- 1 small pkg. prepared herb stuffing mix
- ¼ C. butter or margarine

Arrange broccoli in bottom of greased 9x13-inch baking dish. Arrange ham and eggs, yolk side up, on broccoli. Blend soup and milk together until smooth; spoon over each egg. Combine stuffing mix, butter and cider; sprinkle over casserole. Bake uncovered at 350° for 45 minutes to 1 hour. Can be made up a day ahead and baked next day. Yield: 10-12 servings.

BAR-B-Q BEEF

4 lb. pot roast
1 can tomato soup
1 bottle catsup (small)
1 C. cider
2 T. lemon juice
2 T. Worcestershire sauce

2 T. brown sugar
½ tsp. dry mustard
1 medium onion
½ C. chopped celery
4 bay leaves (if desired)
Salt and pepper to taste

Cover roast with cider. Cook slowly for a long time until tender. Remove meat. Cool broth and skim off fat. Shred the meat and combine with remaining ingredients and broth. Simmer slowly until cooked down and good texture (1 hour) for sandwich making. Enough for 20 sandwiches. Freezes well.

CROCK POT STUFFING

- 1 C. margarine
- 2 C. chopped onion
- 2 C. chopped celery
- 2 (8 oz. ea.) cans mushrooms (drained)
- 1 can cream of mushroom soup diluted with 1 can cider
- 12-13 C. seasoned dry bread crumbs
- 1½ tsp. salt
- 2 well beaten eggs
- 3½-4½ C. broth

Melt butter (margarine); saute onion, celery and mushrooms in butter. Pour over bread crumbs in large mixing bowl. Toss well. Pour in enough broth to moisten well; add eggs and mix. Add remaining broth. Pack lightly into crock pot. Cover and set on high for 45 minutes. Reduce to low for 6-8 hours. (You can make this the day before a holiday.)

HAMBURGER AND RICE CASSEROLE DISH

1 C. uncooked rice (not the quick kind)
1½ lbs. hamburger
2 cans cream of chicken soup
2 cans cider
Small onion

Cook hamburger and onion until done but not brown - add other ingredients and bake in 7½x12-inch Pyrex for 2 hours at 300°. Stir every ½ hour. One-half hour before removing from oven, add buttered bread crumbs or crushed potato chips. Can use 3 C. diced chicken or turkey instead of hamburger.

SALADS

Angel Food Dessert — 131
Blueberry Salad — 129
Broken Glass Dessert — 127
Caribbean Chicken Salad — 111
Cinnamon Apple Salad — 123

Crock Salad	128
Diet Coleslaw Dressing	130
Frozen Fruit Cup	132
Grapefruit Sorbet	121
Hot Dried Beef Potato Salad	119
Lemon Salad	117
Rhubarb Crunch	125
Rigatoni Salad	113
Tapioca Pudding Salad	115

Caribbean Chicken Salad

DRESSING:
1/2 c. plain nonfat yogurt

SALAD:
16 oz. chicken breast strips
3/4 c. apple juice
3/4 c. water
1/2 c. long grain & wild rice, uncooked
3/4 c. McIntosh apple, unpeeled & chopped

1/4 c. light mayonnaise
1/4 tsp. cinnamon

1/2 c. celery, sliced
1/2 c. water chestnuts, chopped
30 seedless green grapes, cut into halves
Spinach leaves to garnish (optional)

1. Cook rice according to package directions.
2. Wash chicken pieces; pat dry. Set aside.
3. To prepare dressing, combine all ingredients in a small bowl; cover and refrigerate.
4. In a 2-quart saucepan, simmer chicken, apple juice and water, covered, over medium heat 15 to 20 minutes until juice runs clear when meat is pierced with fork. Remove chicken from pan and reserve juices for cooking rice.
5. Cut chicken in half-inch cubes; cover and chill.
6. Cook long grain and wild rice in cooking juices from chicken, adding water as needed, following label directions.
7. In a large bowl, gently toss together rice, apple, celery, water chestnuts and grapes; stir in chicken and dressing.
8. Serve on spinach leaves.

RIGATONI SALAD

Cook 16 oz. rigatoni 17 minutes, (watch time).
Rinse with hot water. Mix and heat the following:

2 c. sugar	2 c. vinegar
1 c. cider	4 tsp. salt
1 c. Mazola oil (opt)	

Add:

1 chopped onion   1/2 c. chopped green pepper
1/4 c. chopped pimento
Marinate 24 hours. You may also use garlic salt and/or celery seed. Keeps good for several days.

TAPIOCA PUDDING SALAD

2 pkg. instant tapioca pudding
1 (3 oz) box orange jello
3 c. boiling cider

Mix together and set in refrigerator to cool, stirring occasionally. When almost set, add:

1 (8 oz) container Cool Whip
2 cans Mandarin oranges
nuts, if desired

Refrigerate until set. Serve.

LEMON SALAD

1 pkg. lemon jello 2 c. hot cider
3 bananas, cut up 12 large marshmallows, cut up
1 large can crushed pineapple, drained, save juice

TOPPING:
1 c. pineapple juice (add water) 2 eggs, beaten
1/2 c. sugar dash of salt
2 tbsp. flour 1 pint whipped cream

Prepare jello. Add bananas, marshmallows and pineapple. Put in a 9 x 13 pan. Cook topping ingredients (except whipped cream). Cool and spread over chilled jello mixture. Spread whipped cream over all. Chill.

HOT DRIED BEEF POTATO SALAD

2 T. butter
2 T. finely chopped onion
1 tsp. finely chopped green pepper
3 T. water
¼ C. cider vinegar

1 T. sugar
1½ tsp. flour
1 T. cider
1 (¼ lb.) pkg. dried beef
2 C. boiled cubed potatoes

Melt butter in skillet. Add onions and green peppers. Simmer until onions become transparent. Add 3 T. water, vinegar and sugar. Mix well, then slowly add flour which has been blended with the 1 T. cider. Stir until mixture thickens. Cut ½ of the dried beef into small pieces, saving larger slices. Cover cut portions with boiling water and drain immediately. Add cut dried beef and potatoes to seasonings in skillet. Mix thoroughly. Arrange hot salad on platter and surround with remaining slices of dried beef.

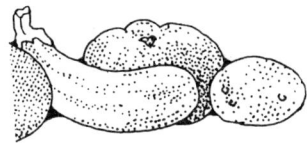

GRAPEFRUIT SORBET

½ C. sugar
1 C. cider
1 (6¼ oz.) can frozen
  concentrated grapefruit juice

Grated rind and juice of one
  grapefruit
2 egg whites

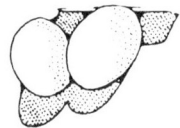

Place sugar and cider in a saucepan. Stir over low heat until sugar has dissolved. Increase heat and boil for 1 minute without stirring, then remove from heat and allow to get cold. Add concentrated juice and rind and juice of grapefruit to the syrup and pour into a shallow rigid container. Freeze for 1 hour or until the sorbet is just beginning to reach a mushy stage. Turn mixture into a bowl and beat until smooth. Whisk egg whites until stiff and fold into sorbet. Return to container. Cover, seal and return to freezer. To Serve: Thaw, covered, in the refrigerator for 10 minutes. Serves 6.

CINNAMON APPLE SALAD

1 pkg. lemon jello
3/4 c. cider
1 pkg. cream cheese
1/4 c. nuts

1 c. red hots
2 c. applesauce
dash of salt
small amount of cream

Boil and stir red hots in cider until dissolved. Add jello and applesauce. Mix. Divide mixture in half and place in a loaf pan. Refrigerate until set. Mix the cream cheese, salt, nuts and cream together until smooth. Spread on jelled half. Pour other half of jello on top and refrigerate again till set.

RHUBARB CRUNCH

1 C. flour
¾ C. oatmeal (uncooked)
1 C. brown sugar
½ C. melted oleo
1 tsp. cinnamon

4 C. diced rhubarb
1 C. white sugar
1 C. cider
1 tsp. vanilla
2 T. cornstarch

Mix flour and oatmeal, brown sugar, shortening and cinnamon until crunchy. Press half of mixture into greased 9-inch pan. Put rhubarb in pan over crumb mixture. Combine white sugar, cider, vanilla and cornstarch. Cook over low heat until thick and clear. Pour over rhubarb and top with remaining crumbs. Bake in moderate oven, 350° for 1 hour. Serve warm or cold with ice cream.

BROKEN GLASS DESSERT

3 pkgs. Jello (lemon, lime and raspberry)

1½ C. hot cider to each and pour into 3 flat pans

Cool and cut into cubes.

HEAT:
1 C. pineapple or orange juice
½ C. sugar

1 pkg. gelatine and
¼ C. cold cider

Then cool. Whip 1 C. whipping cream, ½ C. sugar and lemon flavoring. Fold in plain gelatine and Jello cubes. Turn into graham cracker crust and chill.

CROCK SALAD

1 large head cabbage
2 large carrots (grated)
Celery and onions to taste
1 red or green pepper

2 C. sugar
2 C. vinegar
2 T. white mustard seed
2 T. celery seed

BRINE:
1 gal. cider

1 T. salt

Chop the vegetables, pour brine over them. Place in a crock and let stand overnight in refrigerator (covered). Make syrup of sugar, vinegar, celery seed and mustard seed. Bring solution to boil and let cool. Pour brine off vegetables and put syrup over them. Place in covered container and serve as needed. Keep in refrigerator.

BLUEBERRY SALAD

2 pkg. grape jello
1 can blueberry pie filling
1 (3 oz) pkg. cream cheese
3 c. boiling cider
1 c. cool whip

Dissolve jello in boiling cider . When partially set, add blueberry pie filling. Let set until firm. Top with Cool Whip into which cream cheese has been blended. Top with nuts. May be served as a salad or a dessert.

DIET COLESLAW DRESSING

3/4 c. plain low fat yogurt
1/3 c. red wine vinegar
1/4 c. cider
4 packets of Equal
1/4 tsp. salt
Dash of pepper

Combine all ingredients in bowl and beat with wire whisk. Chill. Note: 7 calories per tablespoon.

ANGEL FOOD DESSERT

Angel food cake
2 boxes strawberry Jello
3 C. hot cider

2 (10 oz. ea.) boxes frozen strawberries
1 pint whipping cream (whipped)

Mix strawberry Jello with hot cider and cool. Combine 2 boxes strawberries and 1 pint whipping cream which has been whipped. Combine whipped cream mixture with Jello. Pour over pieces of angel food cake, broken in a 9x13-inch pan. Refrigerate. You may use raspberries and raspberry Jello.

FROZEN FRUIT CUP

2 boxes frozen strawberries
1 (No. 2) can pineapple tidbits
   or crushed pineapple
   (juice included)

1 (No. 2) can apricots (drained
   and sliced)
4-5 mashed bananas
2 C. sugar
1 C. cider

Boil sugar and cider and pour over strawberries. After strawberries are thawed, mix with the rest of ingredients and freeze in individual cups. Take from freezer 2 hours before serving.

BREADS

Angel Biscuits	137
Danish Puff	141
Lemon Poppy Seed Bread	139
Oatmeal Bread	143
Strawberry Nut Bread	145
Whole Wheat Honey Bread	134

WHOLE WHEAT HONEY BREAD

2 pkg. active dry yeast
2/3 c. nonfat dry milk powder
1/2 c. all-purpose flour
1-1/2 tsp. salt
1/4 c. honey
5-1/2 to 5-3/4 c. whole wheat flour
2-1/2 c. warm cider (110 - 115 degrees)
1/2 c. soy flour, optional
1/2 c. cooking oil
1 egg

In a large bowl dissolve yeast in warm cider. Stir in nonfat dry milk powder, all-purpose flour (use 2/3 c. if not using soy flour), soy flour if desired, and salt. Combine oil, honey, and egg; add to yeast mixture. Beat well by hand. Stir in as much of the whole wheat flour as you can mix in with a spoon. Turn dough out onto a lightly floured surface; knead in enough of the remaining whole wheat flour to make a stiff dough. Continue kneading 5 to 8 minutes or till smooth and elastic.

Place dough in a large, greased bowl, turning once to grease surface. Cover; let rise in a warm place about 1 hour or till nearly double. Punch down. On a lightly floured surface, divide dough in half.

Shape into two loaves. **Place loaves, seam side down, in two greased 9 x 5 x 3 loaf pans. Cover; let rise in a warm place about 45 minutes or till nearly double. Bake in a 350 degree oven for 35-40 minutes, or till loaves sound hollow when lightly tapped (cover loaves with foil the last 10 minutes to prevent over browning).
Immediately turn out onto wire racks; cool. Makes 2 loaves.

ANGEL BISCUITS

5 cups flour
1 tsp. salt
1/2 cup shortening
2 tbsp. warm cider

1 tsp. soda
3 tbsp. sugar
1 package yeast
2 cups buttermilk

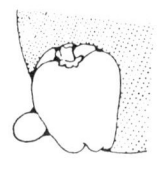

Dissolve yeast in 2 tbsp. warm cider. Add to buttermilk. Sift flour, soda, salt and sugar into mixing bowl. Work shortening into flour mixture. Mix in milk. Roll out to 1/2

inch thickness on a floured board. Melt some butter in baking pan. Dip biscuits in butter. Let rise in a warm place for 1/2 hour. Bake until nicely browned in a 450 degree oven.

*Buttermilk (1 3/4 cup milk and 4 tbsp. vinegar))

LEMON POPPY SEED BREAD

4 eggs; slightly beaten
1 box Betty Crocker lemon or yellow cake mix
1 cup cider
sm. pkg. instant lemon or coconut pudding
1/2 cup oleo (softened)
1/4 cup poppy seed

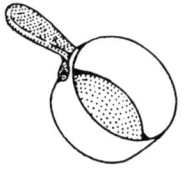

Mix everything together except poppy seed. Blend at medium speed 4 minutes. Fold in poppy seed last. Divide into greased and floured loaf pans. Bake 350 degrees for 45 minutes.

DANISH PUFF

1 C. oleo (2 sticks)
2 C. sifted flour
¼ tsp. salt
2 T. cold cider

1 C. boiling water
2 tsp. almond flavoring
3 eggs
Powdered sugar icing

Cut ½ C. of the oleo into 1 C. flour and the salt until it resembles coarse meal. Add cold cider and stir until well blended. Divide dough in half and

press each half into a 3x12-inch oblong on an ungreased baking sheet. Place boiling water and other ½ C. oleo in saucepan. Bring to a boil. When oleo is melted, add almond flavoring and remove from heat. Immediately stir in other cup of flour. Beat mixture until smooth and add eggs, one at a time. Beat well after each addition. Spread mixture over the pie pastry. Bake at 425° for about 50 minutes. Frost cakes while hot. Cut into slices and serve warm.

For Powdered Sugar Icing: Combine following ingredients and beat until smooth: 2 C. sifted powdered sugar, 1 T. butter, 3 T. milk, 1 tsp. vanilla and 1/8 tsp. salt.

OATMEAL BREAD

2 c. oats
1 tbsp. salt
1 tbsp. sugar
5 c. boiling cider
1 pkg. yeast
1/4 c. lukewarm water
1/3 c. brown sugar
3 c. lukewarm water
15 c. flour

Mix oats, salt and sugar. Add boiling cider and let stand until warm. Mix yeast in 1/4 c. water and let stand 5 minutes. Stir into oats and beat 1 minute. Rise 1 hour. Dissolve brown sugar in 1 c. water. Stir into oats and add 2 c. water. Stir in as much flour as possible. Turn onto floured board and work in rest of flour, knead for 5 minutes. Dough should be soft. Let rise until double. Turn out and knead briefly. Shape into loaves and put in greased pans. Cover and let rise 30 minutes. Bake 10 minutes at 400 degrees, then 45 minutes at 350 degrees. Makes 6 loaves.

Strawberry Nut Bread

1 1/2 c. fresh strawberries;
   or frozen unsweetened
   & defrosted strawberries
1 3/4 c. flour
1 tsp. baking soda
1/4 tsp. baking powder
3/4 tsp. salt
1/2 tsp. cinnamon
1 c. sugar

1/4 c. vegetable oil
1/2 c. egg substitute or
   4 egg whites
1/3 c. cider
1/4 c. walnuts, chopped
2 c. fresh strawberries
   (optional)
Nonstick vegetable
   cooking spray

1. Purée 1 1/2 cups strawberries in blender to yield 1 cup.
2. Combine flour, baking soda, baking powder, salt and cinnamon in a

large mixing bowl.
3. Blend sugar, oil and egg substitute until light and fluffy.
4. Alternately add flour mixture and cider to creamed mixture, mixing at low speed of electric mixer.
5. Stir in puréed strawberries; fold in walnuts.
6. Spread batter in a 9x5-inch loaf pan that has been sprayed with cooking spray.
7. Bake at 350°F. for about 1 hour or until toothpick inserted in center comes out clean.
8. Cool in pan 10 minutes; remove from pan and cool completely on wire rack.
9. Slice bread into 16 servings and serve with fresh strawberries if desired.

CAKE & PIE

Apple Crisp	153
Butterscotch Pie	164
Chocolate Buttermilk Cake	162
Chocolate Mousse Celebration Cake	148
Crazy Cake	166
Lazy Day Pie	160
Lemon Loaf Cake	159
Miracle Whip Cake	163
Never Fail Meringue	161
One Bowl Chocolate Cake	165
Peach Pie	154
Rice Cake	151
Swedish Tea Ring	157
White Texas Sheet Cake	155

CHOCOLATE MOUSSE CELEBRATION CAKE

1 (14 oz) can Eagle brand sweetened
condensed milk (not evaporated milk)
1 (4-serving size) chocolate flavor pudding mix (not instant)
1 c. cider   3 eggs plus 1 egg yolk
1 (1 oz) square unsweetened chocolate
2-2/3 c. all-purpose flour
1 tbsp. baking powder   1-1/3 c. sugar
1/2 c. crisco shortening   2 tsp. vanilla

1 c. milk
1 c. (1/2 pint) whipping cream, stiffly whipped

Preheat oven to 350 degrees. In medium saucepan, combine sweetened condensed milk, cider, pudding mix and 1 egg yolk; mix well. Add chocolate. Over medium heat, cook and stir until mixture boils and thickens. Cool 20 minutes. Beat until smooth. Chill thoroughly, at least 1-1/2 hours. Meanwhile, combine flour and baking powder. In large bowl, beat sugar, shortening and vanilla until well blended. Add 3 eggs, 1 at a time, beating well after each addition. Add flour mixture alternately with milk, beating well. Spread into 2 well-greased and floured 9" round layer cake pan. Bake 25 minutes or until wooden pick comes out clean. Cool 10 minutes; remove from pans. Cool completely. Fold whipped cream into chocolate mixture. Place 1 cake layer on serving plate; gently top with half the chocolate mixture. Repeat. Freeze or chill at least 3 hours. Serve frozen or chilled. Store covered in freezer or refrigerator.

RICE CAKE

7 c. cold cider
1 tsp. salt (if salted butter is used, don't use salt)
2 c. rice

Wash rice and cook until soft and all cider is absorbed Remove from stove and add:

1/2 lb. butter or margarine
1/2 lb. cream cheese and mix well

Mix well and take:

1/2 c. sugar
1 c. cold milk or sweet cream
4 eggs
1 c. sifted cake flour or self-rising flour
1 tsp. vanilla

Beat all with a beater and add to rice mixture. Grease and flour pan 13" x 8" x 2". Pour and bake at 375 degrees for one hour or until done.

APPLE CRISP

6-8 apples (4 c. chopped)
1/2 c. oleo
1 c. sugar
1 tsp. cinnamon
3/4 c. flour
1/2 c. cider (or less)

Butter 9" x 13" baking dish - dice apples into dish. Pour cider and cinnamon over apples. Work together sugar, butter, and flour with fork till crumbly. Sprinkle over apples. Bake 30-40 minutes in 350 degree oven till browned on top.

PEACH PIE

2 cups peaches sliced
1/2 pkg. orange flavored gelatin
3/4 cup boiling cider
Chill until slightly thickened, then pour into chilled crust.
Crust
1 cup finely crushed graham crackers
3 tbsp. powdered sugar
4 tbsp. butter
Mix thoroughly and pat into pan. Chill.

WHITE TEXAS SHEET CAKE

2 sticks oleo
2 c. plus 2 tsp. flour
3 eggs
1 tsp. soda
1 tsp. vanilla
1 c. cider
2 c. sugar
1/2 c. buttermilk
1 tsp. salt

Bring 2 sticks oleo, 1 c. cider to rolling boil and pour over flour and sugar. Mix well, adding 1/2 c. buttermilk, 1 tsp. soda, 1 tsp. salt, 1 tsp. vanilla; add 3 eggs. Beat. Bake in jelly roll pan in 375 degree oven for 20 minutes. Frost while warm with 1 stick oleo, melted, 1/4 c. milk, 1 tsp. vanilla, 1 lb. box of powdered sugar.

SWEDISH TEA RING

2 pkgs. granulat yeast
¼ C. lukewarm cider
¾ C. milk
½ C. sugar
1 tsp. salt
2 eggs
½ C. soft shortening

1 tsp. lemon rind
4½ C. sifted all-purpose flour
2 T. melted butter
⅓ C. sugar
1 tsp. cinnamon
½ C. seedless raisins
¼ tsp. nutmeg

Pour cider over yeast and let stand 5 minutes. Heat milk to lukewarm, add sugar, salt, eggs, shortening and lemon rind. Add 2 C. flour, beat well. Add remaining flour, turn dough out on lightly floured board and knead until smooth. Place dough in greased bowl, cover, set in warm place (80°-85°)

until double in size, 1¼-1½ hours. Press 2 fingers in dough, punch down, let rise again until almost doubled in bulk. Roll dough into oblong 10x20-inch, spread with melted butter and sprinkle with sugar mixed with cinnamon, nutmeg and raisins. Roll up tightly, beginning at the divided side. Pinch edges together, place sealed edges down in ring on cookie sheet, join edges and seal. With scissors make cuts ⅔ way down the ring at 1-inch intervals. Turn each section on its side, let rise until doubled in bulk, about 30-40 minutes. Bake in 350° oven for 40 minutes and frost with ½ C. confectioner's sugar, 1 T. hot water, ½ tsp. vanilla extract. Decorate with nuts and cherries. A good holiday treat you will enjoy.

LEMON LOAF CAKE

1 pkg. yellow cake mix
4 whole eggs
3/4 c. oil

1 pkg. lemon gelatin
3/4 c. cider

Mix all ingredients together. Bake according to cake mix until done. When done, put holes in hot cake. Combine the following: 2 c. sifted powdered sugar, 2 tbsp. butter, 4 or 5 tbsp. lemon juice and pour over cake while hot.

LAZY DAY PIE

1 quart sweetened peaches
1/2 cup cider
3/4 cup sugar

1 stick butter (1/2 cup)
3/4 cup flour

Melt butter in a 1 1/2 quart baking dish. Mix together sugar, flour and cider. Pour over butter. Place peaches on top. Bake in 425 degree oven for 30 minutes or until crust is done.

NEVER FAIL MERINGUE

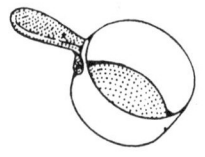

3 egg whites at room temperature
6 tbsp. sugar
1/2 cup cold cider
1 tbsp. cornstarch

Cook cornstarch and cold cider until clear. Let cool. Beat egg whites until they form peaks. Add sugar, 1 tbsp. at a time while continuing beating. Add cooked cornstarch and beat well.

Chocolate Buttermilk Cake

2 c. sugar
3 c. flour
6 T. cocoa powder
2 tsp. baking soda
1 tsp. salt

1 tsp. vanilla
1/4 c. vegetable oil
2 c. cold cider
3/4 c. low-fat buttermilk

1. Preheat oven to 350°F.
2. Combine sugar, flour, cocoa powder, baking soda and salt.
3. Add remaining ingredients.
4. Pour into a small pan. Bake for 25 to 30 minutes.

MIRACLE WHIP CAKE

Preheat oven to 350 degrees. Mix together:

2 c. sifted flour	1 c. sugar
4 tbsp. cocoa	2 tsp. baking soda
1 c. hot cider	1 c. Miracle Whip
1 tsp. vanilla	

Bake for 30 - 40 minutes

BUTTERSCOTCH PIE

1 cup brown sugar
2 tbsp. flour
2 tbsp. butter
2 egg yolks
1 tsp. vanilla
1 cup warm cider

Mix flour, sugar, beaten egg yolks, and warm cider together. Cook until thick. Stir constantly. When cold add vanilla and put into baked pie shell. Chill. Serve with whipped cream.

ONE BOWL CHOCOLATE CAKE

1 c. sugar	1-1/2 c. flour
1/2 c. shortening	1 tsp. baking soda
1 egg	1/2 tsp. salt
1/2 c. cocoa	1/2 c. milk
1 tsp. vanilla	1/2 c. boiling cider

Sift flour with salt and soda. Mix all the ingredients together and beat hard for 3 minutes. Pour into greased pan and bake at 350 degrees for 35-40 minutes. Cool and frost.

CRAZY CAKE

3/4 c. salad oil
2 tsp. vinegar
1 tsp. vanilla
2 c. cider
3 c. flour

2 c. sugar
2 tsp. soda
1/3 c. cocoa
1 tsp. salt

Preheat oven to 350 degrees. Mix all together and put into 9" x 13" ungreased pan. Bake for 35-40 minutes.

MISC.

Baked Ham Glazes	169
Date Filling	168
Easy Meat Sauce	170
Pumpkin Mousse	171

DATE FILLING

1 lb. cut-up dates
1 c. sugar
1 c. cider

Cook over low heat to the consistency of jam.

BAKED HAM GLAZES

1. 1 c. brown sugar, juice and rind of one orange
2. 1 c. honey
3. 1 c. pureed apricots, rhubarb or applesauce
4. 1/2 c. maple syrup, 1/2 c. cider and 2 tbsp. mustard
5. 1 glass currant jelly, melted

Easy Meat Sauce

8 oz. 90% lean ground beef
8 oz. lean ground turkey breast
2 (16 oz.) cans spaghetti sauce
1 c. cider
2 T. Italian herb seasonings blend

1. Heat skillet on stove for 3 to 5 minutes.
2. When hot, add ground meats and brown; drain off fat.
3. Add spaghetti sauce, cider and seasonings.
4. Simmer 30 to 45 minutes.
5. Serve over spaghetti for a wonderful meal.

Pumpkin Mousse

1/4 c. cold cider	1 1/2 tsp. cinnamon or
1 env. plain gelatin	pumpkin spice
1 c. canned pumpkin,	1 tsp. vanilla
warmed	1 pt. vanilla ice milk

1. Place cider and gelatin in blender to soften for 5 minutes.
2. Add pumpkin, spice and vanilla. Blend well.

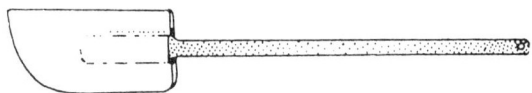

3. Gradually add ice milk.
4. Pour into 4 dessert dishes and chill until firm.

Yield: 4 servings
Per Serving:
   122 cal, 3 gm fat, 5 gm pro, 20 carb, 9 mg chol, 55 mg sodium, 1 gm dietary fiber

Are you up a stump for some nice gifts for some nice people in your life? Well, don't forget HEARTS'N TUMMIES COOKBOOKS. Here's a list of some of the best cookbooks in the western half of the Universe. Just check 'em off, stick a check in an envelope with this page, and we'll get your books off to you pronto. Oh, yes, add $2.00 for shipping and handling. If you order over $25.00 worth, forget the shipping and handling.

Here they are! Mini Cookbooks

(Only 3-1/2 x 5) With Maxi Good Eatin' - 160 or 192 pages - $5.95

- ☐ Arkansas Cooking
- ☐ Dakota Cooking
- ☐ Illinois Cooking
- ☐ Indiana Cooking
- ☐ Iowa Cookin'
- ☐ Kansas Cookin'
- ☐ Michigan Cooking
- ☐ Minnesota Cookin'
- ☐ Missouri Cookin'
- ☐ New Jersey Cooking
- ☐ New York Cooking
- ☐ Ohio Cooking
- ☐ Pennsylvania Cooking
- ☐ Wisconsin Cooking
- ☐ Aphrodisiac Cooking
- ☐ Apples! Apples! Apples!
- ☐ Apples Galore
- ☐ Berries! Berries! Berries!
- ☐ Cherries! Cherries! Cherries!
- ☐ Citrus! Citrus! Citrus!
- ☐ Cooking with Fresh Herbs
- ☐ Cooking with Spirits
- ☐ Cooking with Garlic
- ☐ Cooking with Things Go Cluck
- ☐ Cooking with Things Go Moo
- ☐ Cooking with Things Go Oink
- ☐ Cooking with Things Go Splash
- ☐ Cape Cod Cooking
- ☐ Good Cookin' From the Plain People
- ☐ Hill Country Cookin'
- ☐ Kid Cookin'
- ☐ The Kid's Garden Fun Book
- ☐ Kid Pumpkin Fun Book
- ☐ Midwest Small Town Cookin'
- ☐ Muffins Cookbook
- ☐ Nuts! Nuts! Nuts!
- ☐ Off To College Cookbook
- ☐ Peaches! Peaches! Peaches!
- ☐ Pregnant Lady Cooking
- ☐ Pumpkins! Pumpkins! Pumpkins!

- ☐ Super Simple Cookin'
- ☐ Working Girl Cookbook
- ☐ Veggie Talk Coloring & Story Book $6.95

In Between Cookbooks
(5 1/2 x 8 1/2) - 150 pages - $9.95

- ☐ The Adaptable Apple Cookbook
- ☐ Breads! Breads! Breads!
- ☐ Camp Cookin'
- ☐ Cooking Ala Nude
- ☐ The Cow Puncher's Cookbook
- ☐ Eating Ohio
- ☐ Farmers Market Cookbook
- ☐ The Fire Fighters Cookbook
- ☐ Halloween Fun Book
- ☐ Herbal Cookery
- ☐ Hunting in the Nude Cookbook
- ☐ Ice Cream Cookbook
- ☐ Wil-kon-ge Inizan Maazina 'Igans (The Indian Moon Cookbook)
- ☐ Indian Cooking Cookbook
- ☐ Mad About Garlic
- ☐ Motorcycler's Wild Critter Cookbook
- ☐ Soccer Mom's Cookbook
- ☐ Shhhh Cookbook
- ☐ Vegan Vegetarian Cookbook

Biggie Cookbooks
(5-1/2 x 8-1/2) - 200 plus pages - $11.95

- ☐ A Cookbook for them what Ain't Done a Whole lot of Cookin'
- ☐ Aphrodisiac Cooking
- ☐ Back to the Supper Table Cookbook
- ☐ Cooking for One (ok, Maybe two)
- ☐ Covered Bridges Cookbook
- ☐ Depression Times Cookbook
- ☐ Dial-a-Dream Cookbook
- ☐ Flat out, Dirt Cheap Cookin'
- ☐ Hormone Helper Cookbook
- ☐ The I-got-Funner-things-to-do-than-cook Cookbook
- ☐ Lake Country Cookbook
- ☐ Mississippi River Cookin'
- ☐ The Orchard, Berry Patches and Gardens Cookbook
- ☐ Roarin' 20's Cookbook
- ☐ Wild Critter Cookbook

☐ The Body Shop (A Low-Fat Cookbook) $14.95

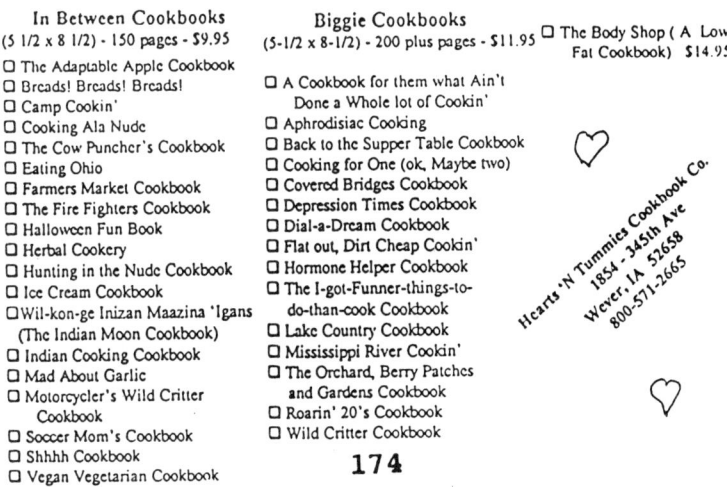

Hearts 'N Tummies Cookbook Co.
1854 - 345th Ave
Wever, IA 52658
800-571-2665

175